Let's Visit the Moon

written by Ben Farrell
illustrated by Bernard Most

HARCOURT BRACE & COMPANY

Orlando   Atlanta   Austin   Boston   San Francisco   Chicago   Dallas   New York
Toronto   London

What will we wear on the moon?

We'll wear space suits like these.

Can we land on the moon?

Yes. There are many places to land.

Will it be hot on the moon?

Yes. The heat comes from the sun.

Will it be cold on the moon?
Yes. The moon is cold at night.

Is the sky blue on the moon?
No. The sky is black on the moon.

What is on the moon?

A lot of rocks!

Will we stay on the moon long?

No. The moon has no air.

Will it take long to get home?
Yes. The Earth is far from the moon.